SCHOLASTIC

Vocabulary Packets

No More Overused Words

by Liane B. Onish

NEW YORK • TORONTO • LONDON • AUCKLAND • SYDNEY
MEXICO CITY • NEW DELHI • HONG KONG • BUENOS AIRES

Hi, Mom!
Thanks, Sarah!

Edited by Sarah Longhi
Content editing by Eileen Judge
Cover design by Ka-Yeon Kim
Interior design by Brian LaRossa

ISBN-13: 978-0-545-19863-9
ISBN-10: 0-545-19863-1
Copyright © 2010 by Liane B. Onish.
All rights reserved. Published by Scholastic Inc.
Printed in the U.S.A.

1 2 3 4 5 6 7 8 9 10   40   16 15 14 13 12 11 10

Contents

Introduction

The goal of *Vocabulary Packets: No More Overused Words* is to introduce, reinforce, and provide practice with interesting synonyms for commonly overused words. The activities are game-oriented to make learning new words fun. Students will have multiple encounters with each synonym to reinforce learning so they can "own" their new knowledge. Each unit features engaging activities students can do over the course of several days. Students will use clues to discover hidden common words in definitions of synonyms, complete cloze sentences and a crossword puzzle, make their own Word Cards with the synonyms and other related words they know, and then use the synonyms to play word games. The rewards are the "ah-ha" moments as learners gain a deeper understanding of individual and related words.

What the Research Says

Words are the name of the game. The more words you know, the more words you can speak, read, and write. Since we use words to think, the more words we know, the finer our understanding of the world is. The more students read, the more new words they will encounter repeatedly and learn (National Reading Panel, 2003). Therefore literacy programs should incorporate the following principles:

- ► Students must have multiple encounters with new words for them to affect comprehension and become a permanent addition to vocabulary.
  (Stahl & Fairbanks, 1986).

- ► Instructional design should include frequent encounters with new words, richness of instruction, and extension of word use beyond the classroom.
  (Beck, McKeown, Kucan, 2002).

- ► Explicit instruction of academic words "yields a great return because students will repeatedly encounter these words throughout reading in content areas across the grades." (Dr. Kate Kinsella, 2005, as cited in READ 180 Rbook stage C TE pT72).

- ► Effective vocabulary instruction uses familiar language to explain word meanings, meaningful examples, and ample opportunities to practice (Feldman & Kinsella, 2004).

Vocabulary Packets: No More Overused Words uses related words as well as morphological awareness and meaningful word parts (including prefixes, suffixes and inflectional endings) to increase and deepen vocabulary knowledge.

According to researchers, by the end of high school, the average student knows 80,000 vocabulary words. Only a small percentage of them could have been taught through explicit instruction. There are simply too many words and too little time for a significant number to be directly taught. Giving students strategic tools to deepen their understanding of known words will help them unlock the meaning of new words. *Vocabulary Packets: No More Overused Words* makes learning new words fun and playful—and best of all, it will help make the new vocabulary stick!

How to Use the Book

Vocabulary Packets: No More Overused Words covers 50+ common words and 150+ synonyms. Each unit provides practice with five (or six) words and synonyms over several lessons.

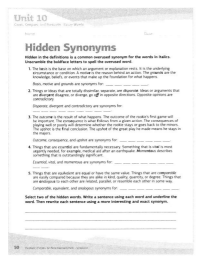

ACTIVITY 1

Hidden Synonyms: Students read clues from three synonyms and their shades of meaning. Embedded in definitions are boldface letters to unscramble that spell a commonly overused word.

ACTIVITY 2

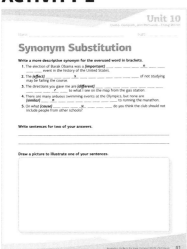

Synonym Substitution: Students supply an interesting synonym for the bracketed common word to complete a cloze sentence. Then students select one of their answers to use in an original sentence and illustration.

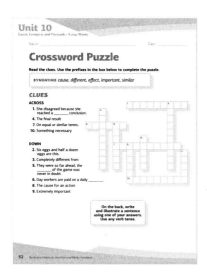

ACTIVITY 3

Crossword Puzzle: Students complete the crossword puzzle with words from the unit. Puzzle clues include definitions, examples, and cloze sentences.

ACTIVITY 4

Student-Made Word Cards: Students complete synonym definitions for the words from the unit. Challenge students to list other synonyms at the bottom of each card. On the back, students write a sentence and illustrate one word.

REVIEW GAMES

After every two units, there is a game to play to review and reinforce word learning. A bonus game follows the review game for units 9 and 10. This bonus game can be played with words from any two units in the book. For additional challenges, use words from more than two units, or add words from other subject areas.

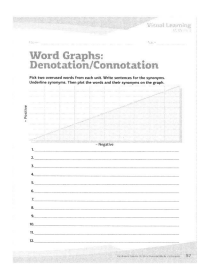

VISUAL LEARNING ACTIVITIES

The book also features three engaging, visually-oriented activities that can be used with one or more units in the book. For one activity, discuss with students the denotation and connotation of word meanings and then have students plot the synonyms on a Word Graph. In another activity, students use sequencing and essay words to move the action in a comic strip. For the third activity, students cut out speech and thought bubbles, as well as boxes for introductory and summary text, which they will add to photographs from newspapers and magazines.

Teaching Tips

▸ Duplicate Unit 1 and staple pages together for each student. As a group, work through the lessons. Encourage students to share their original sentences and drawings. Then have students work on subsequent units independently or with partners, spending five or ten minutes sharing their work in small groups.

▸ Post the overused words and synonyms of the week on chart paper. Have students list synonyms they find in their content area and independent reading on the chart. Students can also add these words to their word cards. Encourage students to use these words to make their own crossword puzzles or cloze sentences for their classmates to solve.

English Language Learners

▸ Review the more familiar synonyms used in the definitions and the activity clues for the target words before introducing each unit. A list of these words can be found on the Master List on pages 8–9.

▸ Use Word Web graphic organizers to explore what students know about the overused words before introducing new synonyms.

▸ Review prefixes *un-*, *dis-*, and *mis-*; suffixes *-able/-ible*, *-less*, *-ful*; and compound words as appropriate.

Master List

UNIT	OVERUSED WORD	SYNONYMS USED IN CLUES	TARGET SYNONYMS
1	answer	reply, state	counter, opine, retort
	ask	beg, plead	beseech, implore, inquire
	say	comment, share, speak, state, add	announce, declare, remark
	tell	admit, state, warn	assert, caution, profess
	yell	holler, shout, utter	bellow, rant, screech
2	awesome	pleasing, finest, terrific	excellent, fabulous, impressive
	awful	dreadful, sad, terrible	dire, horrendous, tragic
	beautiful	attractive, desirable, inviting, lovely	alluring, appealing, exquisite
	perfect	model, lacks defects, without faults, without blemish	flawless, faultless, ideal
	unfair	not equal, uneven	indefensible, inequitable, unwarranted
3	give	present, supply, provide	bestow, equip, furnish
	go	move, follow	advance, ensue, persist
	take	hold, get control of	capture, grasp, seize
	think	thoughtfully consider, have an opinion, judge	contemplate, deem, reflect
	want	strive, desire, wish for	aspire, covet, yearn
4	boring	uninteresting, ordinary, predictable, trite	banal, commonplace, tedious
	get	buy, purchase, sense, become aware of, understand	acquire, obtain, perceive
	like	enjoy, take pleasure in	appreciate, relish, savor
	nice	warm, kind, pleasant, easygoing, good-natured	amiable, congenial, gracious
	very	beyond expectations, extremely	deeply, exceedingly, profoundly
5	bad	horrible, cause dismay	appalling, horrific, injurious
	easy	plain, open, direct, not difficult, simple	straightforward, uncomplicated, undemanding
	good	able, adequate, well	competent, beneficial, respectable
	hard	difficult, impossible	arduous, formidable, problematic
	new	modern, up-to-date, groundbreaking, original	current, innovative, inventive
	old	well known, traditional, adult, out-of-date, not modern	established, mature, passé

Vocabulary Packets: No More Overused Words • Scholastic

UNIT	OVERUSED WORD	SYNONYMS USED IN CLUES	TARGET SYNONYMS
6	dark	brooding, dim, gloomy, up to no good, unsettled	murky, sinister, forbidding
	happy	overjoyed, joyful	elated, euphoric, jubilant
	light	glowing, beaming	incandescent, luminous, radiant
	right	correct	accurate, justified, precise
	sad	feel pain or suffer, full of woe	heartrending, poignant, sorrowful
	wrong	full of errors, defective	erroneous, flawed, misguided
7	hard	stiff, fixed, not easily bent or changed, not giving in	inflexible, rigid, unbending
	rough	uneven, not smooth, not straight or uniform	coarse, irregular, jagged
	smooth	calm, easy to bend, moves with ease or grace, unruffled	consistent, supple, tranquil
	sour	sharp, biting, full of resentment, bad-tempered, nasty	acerbic, disagreeable, embittered
	sweet	sugary, caring, loving, soft	saccharine, sentimental, tender
8	big	large, huge, bulky	gargantuan, immense, massive
	loud	booming, high volume, noisy	deafening, thunderous, vociferous
	small	tiny, miniature, unimportant	diminutive, lilliputian, trivial
	soft	barely audible, light, gentle	delicate, faint, mellow
	tall	great height, huge, raised off the ground	colossal, elevated, lofty
9	about	fairly close, more or less	approximately, approaching, roughly
	first	at the beginning or onset, ahead of others	foremost, initially, originally
	last	end, after all else	conclusive, finally, ultimately
	next	comes after, follows	afterward, following, subsequently
	sometimes	now and then, not often, from time to time	infrequently, occasionally, sporadically
10	cause	base, underlying circumstance or condition, reason	basis, grounds, motive
	different	dissimilar, disagree, opposite	contradictory, disparate, divergent
	effect	result, what follows	consequence, outcome, upshot
	important	necessary, urgently needed	essential, momentous, vital
	similar	equal, same, alike, resemble	analogous, comparable, equivalent

Name _____   Date _____

Hidden Synonyms

Hidden in the definitions is a common overused synonym for the words in italics. Unscramble the boldface letters to spell the overused word.

1. To **a**nnounce is to speak up publicly. To *remark* means to comment or **s**hare a thought. When you *declare* you state something public**ly** and officially.

   Announce, remark, and *declare* are synonyms for ____ ____ ____.

2. When you *assert*, you state firmly. If you *caution*, you warn others. When you *prof**e**ss, you admit something open**ly** and free**ly**.

   Assert, caution, and *profess* are synonyms for ____ ____ ____ ____.

3. When you *inquire*, you politely want to **k**now something. To beg is to *beseech*. If you *implore*, you beg **s**eriously **a**nd sincerely.

   Inquire, beseech, and *implore* are synonyms for ____ ____ ____.

4. To *bellow*, do this **l**oudly. If you *rant*, **y**ou shout loudly and angrily. When you *scr**e**ech*, you utter a **l**oud, high-pitched, shrill sound.

   Bellow, rant, and *screech* are synonyms for ____ ____ ____ ____.

5. To *retort* is to reply sh**a**rply. When you *opine*, you **s**tate your opinion. **W**hen you *count**e**r*, your reply contradicts or opposes what someone else said.

   Retort, opine, and *counter* are synonyms for ____ ____ ____ ____ ____ ____.

Select two of the hidden words. Write a sentence using each word and underline the word. Then rewrite each sentence using a more interesting and exact synonym.

_____

_____

_____

_____

Name _____   Date _____

Synonym Substitution

Write a more descriptive synonym for the overused word in brackets.

1. The little girl *[yelled]* ____ _c_ ____ ____ ____ ____ ____ed when her brother jumped
out of the closet in a monster costume.

2. He *[told]* ____ ____ ____ ____ ____ ____ _n_ ed the team to follow the rules carefully
because this referee liked to called penalties.

3. The committee chairperson *[answered]* ____ ____ ____ ____ ____ _e_ ____ed with
research that proved the opposite.

4. The prisoner would *[say]* ____ ____ ____ _l_ ____ ____ ____d his innocence to anyone
who would listen.

5. Before the camping trip, the scout leader *[asked]* ____ ____ ____ ____ ____ _r_ ____d
if anyone had an allergy to poison ivy lotion.

Write sentences for two of your answers.

_____

_____

Draw a picture to illustrate one of your sentences.

Name _____   Date _____

Crossword Puzzle

Read the clues. Use synonyms for words in the box to complete the puzzle.

> **SYNONYMS** *answer, ask, say, tell, yell*

CLUES

ACROSS

2. The MC _____ the next act.
5. Seriously and sincerely beg
6. State firmly
9. Admit openly and freely for all to hear
10. Holler loudly

DOWN

1. Shout angrily
3. Give an opinion
4. Add a comment or thought
7. To _____ sharply can be like a slap in the face.
8. Plead or beg

> **On the back, write
> and illustrate a sentence
> using one of your answers.
> Use any verb tense.**

Name _____   Date _____

Word Cards

▶ **Write the meaning for each synonym.**

▶ **Add other synonyms for the word.**

▶ **Cut out the cards and tape or staple them to index cards.**

▶ **Write a sentence for one of the synonyms on the back of the card.**

SYNONYMS FOR answer

1. *counter* means _____
2. *retort* means _____
3. *opine* means _____
4. Other words I know for *answer*:

_____

_____

_____

SYNONYMS FOR ask

1. *beseech* means _____
2. *implore* means _____
3. *inquire* means _____
4. Other words I know for *ask*:

_____

_____

_____

SYNONYMS FOR say

1. *announce* means _____
2. *declare* means _____
3. *remark* means _____
4. Other words I know for *say*:

_____

_____

_____

SYNONYMS FOR tell

1. *assert* means _____
2. *caution* means _____
3. *profess* means _____
4. Other words I know for *tell*:

_____

_____

_____

SYNONYMS FOR yell

1. *bellow* means _____
2. *rant* means _____
3. *screech* means _____
4. Other words I know for *yell*:

_____

_____

_____

Name _____   Date _____

Hidden Synonyms

Hidden in the definitions is a common overused synonym for the words in italics. Unscramble the boldface letters to spell the overused word.

1. Something that is *fabulous* is extremely pleasing. That **w**hich is *excellent* is of the highest or finest quality. Something that makes a strong, vivid i**m**pression, one you won't soon forget is *impressiv**e***.

   Fabulous, excellent, and *impressive* are synonyms for

   ____ ____ ____ ____ ____ ____ ____.

2. You like what is attractive and inviting; you **f**ind it *appealing*. Something that is *exquisit**e*** is de**l**icate and intricate in an especially lovely way. What is ***all**uring* is highly attractive and most desira**b**le.

   Appealing, exquisite, and *alluring* are synonyms for

   ____ ____ ____ ____ ____ ____ ____ ____ ____.

3. Something that lacks defe**c**ts or flaws is *f**l**awle**s**s*. If a person is *faul**t**less*, he or she is without blame or faults. When something is *ideal*, it is the model or standa**r**d that **p**eople will strive for.

   Flawless, faultless, and *ideal* are synonyms for ____ ____ ____ ____ ____ ____ ____.

4. A *dire* **w**arning tel**l**s of terrible consequences. A *horrendo**u**s* situation is one that is absolutely dreadf**u**l. A *tra**g**ic* happening is very sad, usually involving death.

   Horrendous, dire, and *tragic* are synonyms for ____ ____ ____ ____ ____.

5. When the sides are not equal, when one group has more players or help than another, the situation is *inequi**t**able*. If someone is completely to blame for an attack, and has no good r**e**ason or defense for his actions, his position is *i**n**defensible*. And if that attack came from out of the blue and was unpro**v**oked, it was also *unwarran**t**ed*.

   Inequitable, indefensible, and *unwarranted* are synonyms for

   ____ ____ ____ ____ ____ ____.

Select two of the hidden words. Write a sentence using each word and underline the word. Then rewrite each sentence using a more interesting and exact synonym.

_____

_____

_____

_____

Name _____   Date _____

Synonym Substitution

Write a more descriptive synonym for the overused word in brackets.

1. The move was a *[awful]* ____ ____ _r_ ____ ____ ____ ____ ____ ____ ____ experience—every single piece of furniture was damaged and several boxes of clothing are still missing.

2. The *[beautiful]* ____ ____ ____ _u_ ____ ____ ____ ____ ____ detail of gold and gems on the tiny pendant must have taken months of painstaking work.

3. When teachers, students, and parents work together, the much improved test scores are *[awesome]* ____ _m_ ____ ____ ____ ____ ____ ____ ____ ____ .

4. How could this *[unfair]* ____ ____ _w_ ____ ____ ____ ____ ____ ____ ____ ____ attack have happened after the peace treaty was signed?

5. It was a *[perfect]* ____ ____ ____ ____ _l_ ____ ____ ____ performance, and the critics were right to give her a rave review.

Write sentences for two of your answers.

_____

_____

Draw a picture to illustrate one of your sentences.

Name _____   Date _____

Crossword Puzzle

Read the clues. Use synonyms for words in the box to complete the puzzle.

> **SYNONYMS** *awesome, beautiful, perfect, awful, unfair*

CLUES

ACROSS

1. That _____ outfit looks terrific!

4. Unfair and uneven

7. Inviting or attractive

8. Having no good reasons for doing something terrible

10. Perfectly suitable

DOWN

2. Highly attractive and desirable

3. Without blemish or flaws

5. An A+ is better than good—it's _____!

6. An accident in which someone dies is this.

9. We evacuated after Earthquake Watch issued _____ warnings.

> **On the back, write and illustrate a sentence using one of your answers. Use any verb tense.**

Name _____   Date _____

Word Cards

- ▸ **Write the meaning for each synonym.**
- ▸ **Add other synonyms for the word.**
- ▸ **Cut out the cards and tape or staple them to index cards.**
- ▸ **Write a sentence for one of the synonyms on the back of the card.**

SYNONYMS FOR *awesome*
1. *impressive* means _____
2. *excellent* means _____
3. *fabulous* means _____
4. Other words I know for *awesome*:

_____

_____

_____

SYNONYMS FOR *beautiful*
1. *appealing* means _____
2. *alluring* means _____
3. *exquisite* means _____
4. Other words I know for *beautiful*:

_____

_____

_____

SYNONYMS FOR *perfect*
1. *flawless* means _____
2. *faultless* means _____
3. *ideal* means _____
4. Other words I know for *perfect*:

_____

_____

_____

SYNONYMS FOR *awful*
1. *dire* means _____
2. *horrendous* means _____
3. *tragic* means _____
4. Other words I know for *awful*:

_____

_____

_____

SYNONYMS FOR *unfair*
1. *inequitable* means _____
2. *unwarranted* means _____
3. *indefensible* means _____
4. Other words I know for *unfair*:

_____

_____

_____

Review Game 1: Story Starters

SKILL Writing sentences and stories
NUMBER OF PLAYERS Pairs or small groups
OBJECT OF THE GAME Use phrases with target words to write group stories
MATERIALS 30 blank word cards (page 62) or index cards; bag

MAKE THE GAME CARDS

1. Make a set of game cards by writing each synonym from units 1 and 2 on individual blank game cards (page 62) or index cards.

2. Place all the word cards in a bag.

PLAY THE GAME

1. Students line up. One by one, they each select a card from the bag, return to their seats, and add a word before or after the synonym (as well as any necessary inflected endings) to make a phrase, for example:

   proudly **announce***d*
   an **excellent** *grade*

2. When they finish their first card, they select a second card and then put the first card back in the bag. If the card they chose has a phrase on it, students add a second phrase.

3. Continue until all cards have three or more phrases on them.

4. Group students in pairs or small groups of 3-5. Have each player pick a card from the bag. Randomly distribute any remaining cards.

5. Groups select favorite phrases from the cards (or write new ones) and use them to write a short story.

6. Encourage groups to share their stories with the class.

Name _____   Date _____

Hidden Synonyms

Hidden in the definitions is a common overused synonym for the words in italics. Unscramble the boldface letters to spell the overused word.

1. To *advance* means to m**o**ve forward. When you *persist*, you keep workin**g** at moving forward or achieving something. To *ensue* means to follow as a result of some other action.

    Advance, persist, and *ensue* are synonyms for ____ ____.

2. When you *grasp* something, you take hold of it. You can grasp an object physically, or grasp an idea intellectually. To *capture* means to put under your control, usually by force. To s**e**ize means to get or control quic**k**ly, sometimes with force. You can seize an opportunity or enemy's ship.

    Grasp, capture, and *seize* are synonyms for ____ ____ ____ ____.

3. To *bestow* means to present as a **g**ift or an honor. To *furnish* means to supply with what is needed, such as furniture. To *equip* means to pro**v**ide needed equipment or supplies.

    Bestow, furnish and *equip* are synonyms for ____ ____ ____ ____.

4. When you **a**spire to something, you **w**ork hard and strive to achieve your goal. You may *year***n** or have a strong desire for something, but that doesn't always mean you're willing to work for it. To *cove**t*** means to wish for longingly, usually for something that belongs to someone else.

    Aspire, yearn, and *covet* are synonyms for ____ ____ ____ ____.

5. *Co*n*template* means one t**h**oughtfully considers an **i**dea or situation. To *deem* means to have an opinion about something or to judge it. When you *reflec**t***, you may spea**k** your carefully considered thoughts or go over them in your mind.

    Contemplate, deem, and *reflect* are synonyms for ____ ____ ____ ____ ____.

Select two of the hidden words. Write a sentence using each word and underline the word. Then rewrite each sentence using a more interesting and exact synonym.

_____

_____

_____

_____

Name _____   Date _____

Synonym Substitution

Write a more descriptive synonym for the overused word in brackets.

1. The president requested that the ten smartest people in the nation
   [think] ____ ____ ____ ____ ____ ____ __p__ ____ ____ ____ ____ the
   problem and report directly to him.

2. The university is planning to *[give]* ____ ____ ____ ____ __o__ ____ an honorary degree
   on the newly elected mayor.

3. Harry Potter and his world have *[taken]* ____ ____ ____ ____ ____ __r__ ____d the
   imagination of a whole generation of children.

4. After successfully completing the first challenge, the red team was able to
   [go] ____ __d__ ____ ____ ____ ____ ____ to the next round.

5. It was a long, cold, miserable winter and everyone *[wanted]* ____ ____ ____ ____ __n__ ed
   for warm spring weather.

Write sentences for two of your answers.

_____

_____

Draw a picture to illustrate one of your sentences.

Name _____   Date _____

Crossword Puzzle

Read the clues. Use synonyms for words in the box to complete the puzzle.

> **SYNONYMS** *go, take, give, want, think*

CLUES

ACROSS

4. To consider thoughtfully

5. Will the dog ever _____ the concept that the dogs on TV can't hear him?

7. After the fire alarm rang, panic _____ .

8. They _____ and strive to win the state championship.

10. To desire something that is not yours

DOWN

1. To judge

2. To make the most of every minute, _____ the day!

3. To supply, especially with household items

6. To get what you want, you may have to do this

9. The grant money will allow us to _____ the lab with new microscopes.

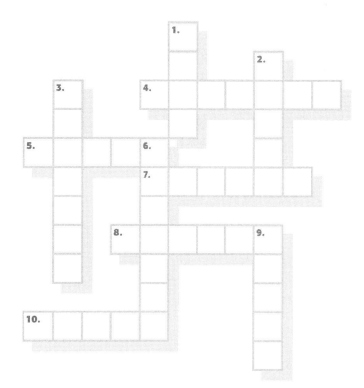

> **On the back, write and illustrate a sentence using one of your answers. Use any verb tense.**

Name _____   Date _____

Word Cards

▸ **Write the meaning for each synonym.**

▸ **Add other synonyms for the word.**

▸ **Cut out the cards and tape or staple them to index cards.**

▸ **Write a sentence for one of the synonyms on the back of the card.**

SYNONYMS FOR go

1. *advance* means _____
2. *ensue* means _____
3. *persist* means _____
4. Other words I know for *go*:

_____

_____

_____

SYNONYMS FOR take

1. *capture* means _____
2. *grasp* means _____
3. *seize* means _____
4. Other words I know for *take*:

_____

_____

_____

SYNONYMS FOR give

1. *bestow* means _____
2. *equip* means _____
3. *furnish* means _____
4. Other words I know for *give*:

_____

_____

_____

SYNONYMS FOR want

1. *aspire* means _____
2. *covet* means _____
3. *yearn* means _____
4. Other words I know for *want*:

_____

_____

_____

SYNONYMS FOR think

1. *contemplate* means _____
2. *deem* means _____
3. *reflect* means _____
4. Other words I know for *think*:

_____

_____

_____

Name _____   Date _____

Hidden Synonyms

Hidden in the definitions is a common overused synonym for the words in italics. Unscramble the boldface letters to spell the overused word.

1. Somethin**g** that is uninte**r**esting, not unusual, or not unexpected is c**o**mm**o**nplace. Something that moves so slowly it seems like it will take forever is t**e**di**o**us. When something is so ordinary, predictable, and trite, it is **b**anal.

   Commonplace, tedious, and *banal* are synonyms for the adjective:
   ____ ____ ____ ____ ____ ____.

2. Someone kind who behaves with grace and elegance is *gracious.* A person who is easy to get along with, friendly, sociable, and good-natured is *amiable.* A pleasant, friendly host who makes sure the guests are comfortable and have everything they need, is *congenial.* Your best friends, who have the same tastes and temperament as you, are also congenial.

   Gracious, amiable, and *congenial* are synonyms for the adjective ____ ____ ____ ____.

3. To *relish* means to take great pleasure in an activity or in a tasty food. To *savor* means to enjoy the taste or smell of something. And when you relish a terrific experience and savor the taste of the world's best pizza, you *appreciate* these things.

   Relish, savor, and *appreciate* are synonyms for the verb ____ ____ ____ ____.

4. When something happens that **r**ocks your world, for good or bad, you feel it *profoundly.* If the experience goes beyond expectations, it is **e**xceedingly or extremely felt. And when something touches you on a deep le**v**el and makes a strong impression, you feel it *deeply.*

   Profoundly, exceedingly, and *deeply* are synonyms for the adverb ____ ____ ____ ____.

5. You *acquire* skills by working hard, and you acquire things by buyin**g** them. You *obtain* results of an experiment or other planned activities. When you *perceive* something, you become aware of and understand it, often using your senses.

   Acquire, obtain, and *perceive* are synonyms for the verb ____ ____ ____.

Select two of the hidden words. Write a sentence using each word and underline the word. Then rewrite each sentence using a more interesting and exact synonym.

_____

_____

_____

_____

Name _____   Date _____

Synonym Substitution

Write a more descriptive synonym for the overused word in brackets.

1. It was a *[nice]* ____ ____ _n_ ____ ____ ____ ____ ____ ____ tea party hosted by the principal for all the new teachers.

2. To show how much they *[liked]* ____ _p_ ____ ____ ____ ____ ____ ____ ____ ___d their coach, the swim team had his whistle gold-plated.

3. Hearing the beautiful voice come out of such an old and feeble body, *[very]* ____ ____ ____ ____ ____ ____ ____ _d_ ____ ____ affected the audience, moving many to tears.

4. The movie was so *[boring]* ____ ____ _d_ ____ ____ ____ ____ that I couldn't stop yawning and my friend fell asleep!

5. So many stores were for rent that we were able to *[get]* ____ _b_ ____ ____ ____ ____ a new lease at a lower rent than last year.

Write sentences for two of your answers.

_____

_____

Draw a picture to illustrate one of your sentences.

Name _____   Date _____

Crossword Puzzle

Read the clues. Use synonyms for words in the box to complete the puzzle.

SYNONYMS *boring, get, like, nice, very*

CLUES

ACROSS

  7. Ordinary

  8. To use one's senses
       to understand

  9. To enjoy every moment

  10. Predictably dull and trite

DOWN

  1. What diners do with every
       bite of a gourmet meal

  2. The tribute to the hero was
       _____ felt by everyone at
       the ceremony.

  3. Above and beyond what is expected

  4. We enjoy going to their home because
       they are such _____ hosts.

  5. To purchase

  6. Easygoing and good-natured

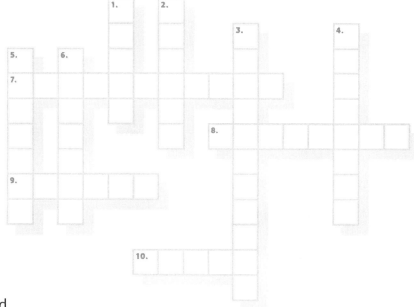

On the back, write
and illustrate a sentence
using one of your answers.
Use any verb tense.

Word Cards

▸ **Write the meaning for each synonym.**

▸ **Add other synonyms for the word.**

▸ **Cut out the cards and tape or staple them to index cards.**

▸ **Write a sentence for one of the synonyms on the back of the card.**

SYNONYMS FOR *boring*

1. *banal* means _____

2. *commonplace* means _____

3. *tedious* means _____

4. Other words I know for *boring*:

_____

_____

_____

SYNONYMS FOR *get*

1. *acquire* means _____

2. *obtain* means _____

3. *perceive* means _____

4. Other words I know for *get*:

_____

_____

_____

SYNONYMS FOR *like*

1. *appreciate* means _____

2. *relish* means _____

3. *savor* means _____

4. Other words I know for *like*:

_____

_____

_____

SYNONYMS FOR *nice*

1. *amiable* means _____

2. *congenial* means _____

3. *gracious* means _____

4. Other words I know for *nice*:

_____

_____

_____

SYNONYMS FOR *very*

1. *deeply* means _____

2. *exceedingly* means _____

3. *profoundly* means _____

4. Other words I know for *very*:

_____

_____

_____

Review Game 2: Synonyms 'Round the Room

SKILL Listing synonyms
NUMBER OF PLAYERS Whole class
OBJECT OF THE GAME To list as many synonyms as possible
MATERIALS 20 sheets of writing paper, 2 different-color markers, timer

PREPARE THE GAME SHEETS

1. Write the ten overused words from Units 3 and 4 at the top of individual sheets of paper in one color marker. Make a second set of those words using the other color.

2. Tape each set of ten pages on the walls of two sides of the classroom. Spread the pages out so students can move easily between them. Students will need their own pen or pencil.

PLAY THE GAME

1. Divide the class into two groups, designated by the color marker used for their team's words.

2. Teams line up in the center of the room.

3. When you say "go," the first player on each team runs to any one of his or her team's game pages. Start the timer. Players have 15 seconds to write one or two synonyms for the word on the page.

4. After 15 seconds, say "go" again, and the next player on each team runs up to the same or a different page. The first player moves to another of his or her team's pages. Teams will get points for each correct synonym.

5. Continue saying "go" every 15 seconds, until all players have had a chance to add a word to his or her team's pages. Remind players to add new words since there are no points for duplications.

6. The team with the most correct synonyms for each word wins.

Name _____   Date _____

Hidden Synonyms

Hidden in the definitions is a common overused synonym for the words in italics. Unscramble the boldface letters to spell the overused word.

1. Someone who is able to **g**et a job **d**one adequately well can be described as competent. When the c**o**mpetent job helps or benefits others, it is *beneficial*. A j**o**b that is well done (though not necessarily perfect) is *respectable*. A respectable person works hard and acts according to the ethics, laws and customs of the culture.

   Competent, beneficial, and *respectable* are synonyms for ____ ____ ____ ____.

2. Something that is **s**traightforward is plain, open and direct. When something is un**de**manding it is not difficult to deal with. A task that is *uncomplic**a**ted* is ver**y** simple, neither complex nor involved.

   Straightforward, undemanding and *uncomplicated* are synonyms for
   ____ ____ ____ ____.

3. A terri**b**le natural disaster that destroys homes and kills people is *horrific*. A crime committed deliberately that causes hurt or injury is *injurious*. News of horrible events, causing dism**a**y, fear, and **d**isgust, is *appalling*.

   Horrific, injurious and *appalling* are synonyms for ____ ____ ____.

4. A very difficult task or type of work is *arduous*. A job t**h**at seems impossible to accomplish is a *formidable* task. Even an easy job can develop unexpected problems and become *proble**m**atic*.

   Arduous, formidable and *problematic* are synonyms for ____ ____ ____ ____.

5. Something that has been around for a long time, that is well known and traditional, is *estab**l**ished*. An adult or person behaving in a grown-up way is *mature*. But a fad or fashion that is **o**ut-of-date and no longer considered modern is *passé*, from the French word meaning "having passed."

   Established, mature and *passé* are synonyms for ____ ____ ____.

6. What is modern and up-to-date is *curr**e**nt*. Something that is groundbreaking and original is *in**n**ovative*. And if the innovation or invention is creative and imaginative as **w**ell as original, it is *inventive*.

   Innovative, current, and *inventive* are synonyms for ____ ____ ____.

On the back of this page, write a sentence using each overused word and underline the word. Then rewrite each sentence using a more interesting and exact synonym.

Name _____   Date _____

Synonym Substitution

Write a more descriptive synonym for the overused word in brackets.

1. My little sister assembled the model by herself because the kit directions were so
   [easy] ____ **t** ____ ____ ____ ____ ____ ____ ____ ____ ____ ____ ____ ____ ____.

2. The president's speech and confidence in the growing economy has a
   [good] ____ ____ **n** ____ ____ ____ ____ ____ ____ ____ effect on the
   stock market.

3. Workers ran into unexpected difficulties, making the repair job more
   [hard] ____ ____ ____ ____ ____ ____ ____ ____ ____ ____ **c** than expected.

4. At graduation, the *[old]* ____ ____ ____ ____ ____ **l** ____ ____ ____ ____ ____
   order is to have the girls and boy march in alphabetically.

5. The *[new]* ____ ____ **r** ____ ____ ____ ____ science fair winners are the younger
   siblings of last year's winners.

6. Eating only fast food and junk food that is full of salt, fat, and sugar is
   [bad] ____ ____ ____ **u** ____ ____ ____ ____ ____ to your health.

Write sentences for two of your answers.

_____

_____

Draw a picture to illustrate one of your sentences.

Name _____   Date _____

Crossword Puzzle

Read the clues. Use synonyms for words in the box to complete the puzzle.

> **SYNONYMS** *bad, easy, good, hard, old, new*

CLUES

ACROSS

2. A turtle is this kind of pet, very easy to care for.

3. Difficult, long, and exhausting

10. Her _____ ideas changed an entire industry.

11. Using imagination to be creative and original

12. The _____ thing to do is walk away from childish name-calling.

DOWN

1. Not difficult or complex

4. Climbing Mt. Everest is a _____ undertaking.

5. So last year!

6. Devastatingly awful

7. Prompting dismay or disgust

8. The B+ she got on her test is certainly a _____ grade.

9. Able to do the task adequately

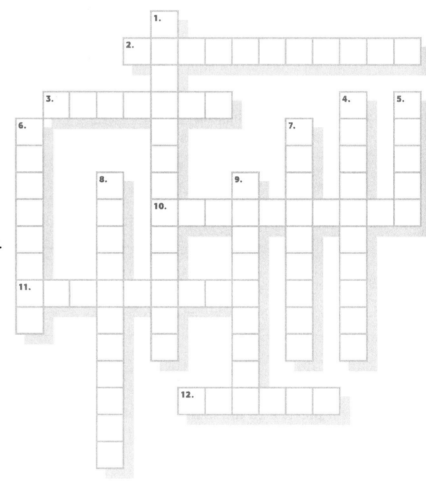

> On the back, write
> and illustrate a sentence
> using one of your answers.
> Use any verb tense.

Name _____   Date _____

Word Cards

Fill in the cards, then cut them out and tape or staple them to index cards. Write a sentence for one of the synonyms on the back of the card.

SYNONYMS FOR *bad*

1. *appalling* means _____
2. *horrific* means _____
3. *injurious* means _____
4. Other words I know for *bad*:

_____
_____
_____

SYNONYMS FOR *easy*

1. *straightforward* means _____
2. *uncomplicated* means _____
3. *undemanding* means _____
4. Other words I know for *easy*:

_____
_____
_____

SYNONYMS FOR *good*

1. *beneficial* means _____
2. *competent* means _____
3. *respectable* means _____
4. Other words I know for *good*:

_____
_____
_____

SYNONYMS FOR *hard*

1. *arduous* means _____
2. *formidable* means _____
3. *problematic* means _____
4. Other words I know for *hard*:

_____
_____
_____

SYNONYMS FOR *new*

1. *current* means _____
2. *innovative* means _____
3. *inventive* means _____
4. Other words I know for *new*:

_____
_____
_____

SYNONYMS FOR *old*

1. *established* means _____
2. *mature* means _____
3. *passé* means _____
4. Other words I know for *old*:

_____
_____
_____

Name _____   Date _____

Hidden Synonyms

Hidden in the definitions is a common overused synonym for the words in italics. Unscramble the boldface letters to spell the overused word.

1. Something that is correct is *accurate* and without errors. If you see an accident, you can give a *precise* description of what **h**appene**d**, explainin**g** clearly what you saw. If you hurt someone in self-defense, it is *jus**t**ifiable.*

   Accurate, precise, and *justifiable* are synonyms for ____ ____ ____ ____ ____.

2. A report that is full of errors is *erro**n**eo**u**s.* A report about a product that is defective or flawed should explain how the item is *flawed.* If a writer is led to believe that a false report will help the company, the writer is *mis**g**uided,* his **w**ork will lead to trouble.

   Erroneous, flawed, and *misguided* are synonyms for ____ ____ ____ ____ ____.

3. The *mur**k**y* light that filters into a basement may be dim and gloomy. A crazed laugh from a ma**d**man's laboratory tells you something evil and *siniste**r*** is about to happen. The man's brooding, *forbidding* manner made all the kids **a**fraid to walk past his house.

   Murky, sinister, and *threatening* are synonyms for ____ ____ ____ ____.

4. The glow from a clock is **l**uminous. Something that is glowin**g** or beaming is *radian**t**.* Intensely **h**appy, joyful people, like a bride and groom on their wedding day, look radiant. *Incandescen**t*** bulbs give off both a bright glow and heat.

   Luminous, radiant and *incandescent* are synonyms for ____ ____ ____ ____ ____.

5. Overjoyed means *el**a**ted.* Championship winners feel *jubilant* both joyful and **p**roud. To be *eu**ph**oric* is to feel jo**y** plus a great sense of well-being.

   Elated, jubilant and *euphoric* are synonyms for ____ ____ ____ ____ ____.

6. To suffer or feel pain from loss or regret is to feel **s**orrowful. Something that is deeply touching or moving, often in a somber or melancholic way, is *poign**a**nt.* Pain that touches the heart and brings out sympathy in others is *heartren**d**ing.*

   Sorrowful, poignant, and *heartrending* are synonyms for ____ ____ ____.

On the back of this page, write a sentence using each overused word and underline the word. Then rewrite each sentence using a more interesting and exact synonym.

Name _____   Date _____

Synonym Substitution

Write a more descriptive synonym for the overused word in brackets.

1. The movie about the poor orphan and his stray dog was so
   [sad] ____ ____ _a_ ____ ____ ____ ____ ____ ____ ____ ____ ____ the entire audience
   was in tears.

2. When peace was declared, people all over the country were so
   [happy] ____ ____ _p_ ____ ____ ____ ____ ____ they danced and shouted for joy, and
   even hugged strangers in the streets.

3. *[dark]* The ____ ____ ____ _b_ ____ ____ ____ ____ ____ ____ look my sister gave me
   warned me not to enter her room!

4. We knew what time it was in the dark movie theater because my watch has a
   [light] ____ ____ ____ _i_ ____ ____ ____ ____ dial.

5. A *[right]* ____ ____ _s_ ____ ____ ____ ____ ____ ____ ____ ____ punishment is one
   that fits the crime.

6. Their conclusion was *[wrong]* ____ ____ ____ ____ ____ ____ ____ _u_ ____ because it
   was based on information that was full of mistakes.

Write sentences for two of your answers.

_____

_____

Draw a picture to illustrate one of your sentences.

Name _____   Date _____

Crossword Puzzle

Read the clues. Use synonyms for words in the box to complete the puzzle.

> **SYNONYMS** *dark, happy, light, sad, right, wrong*

CLUES

ACROSS

3. He gave an _____ summary of the story.
7. The _____ villain was up to no good.
9. Incorrect
10. Joyful
11. Brimming over with happiness
12. Deeply touching and emotionally moving

DOWN

1. Light like a glowing candle
2. Dark, dim, or unclear
4. Full of woe
5. What you are when you get the wrong directions.
6. Correct down to the smallest details
8. The gown was beautiful and her smile was _____.

> **On the back, write and illustrate a sentence using one of your answers. Use any verb tense.**

Name _____   Date _____

Word Cards

Fill in the cards, then cut them out and tape or staple them to index cards. Write a sentence for one of the synonyms on the back of the card.

SYNONYMS FOR *dark*

1. *forbidding* means _____

2. *murky* means _____

3. *sinister* means _____

4. Other words I know for *dark*:

_____

_____

_____

SYNONYMS FOR *light*

1. *incandescent* means _____

2. *luminous* means _____

3. *radiant* means _____

4. Other words I know for *light*:

_____

_____

_____

SYNONYMS FOR *happy*

1. *elated* means _____

2. *euphoric* means _____

3. *jubilant* means _____

4. Other words I know for *happy*:

_____

_____

_____

SYNONYMS FOR *sad*

1. *heartrending* means _____

2. *poignant* means _____

3. *sorrowful* means _____

4. Other words I know for *sad*:

_____

_____

_____

SYNONYMS FOR *right*

1. *accurate* means _____

2. *justifiable* means _____

3. *precise* means _____

4. Other words I know for *right*:

_____

_____

_____

SYNONYMS FOR *wrong*

1. *erroneous* means _____

2. *flawed* means _____

3. *misguided* means _____

4. Other words I know for *wrong*:

_____

_____

_____

Review Game 3: Synonym Slapdown

SKILL Indentifying synonyms
NUMBER OF PLAYERS Groups of 4, 5 or 6 players
OBJECT OF THE GAME To be the first to collect a set of 4 synonym cards
MATERIALS Index cards

MAKE THE GAME CARDS

1. Using index cards, make decks of four synonym cards for each of the words in Units 5 and 6. Write the words along the short side, so the cards are vertical like playing cards. Here is a list of the overused words and their synonyms:

   good, competent, beneficial, respectable
   bad, appalling, injurious, horrific
   easy, straightforward, undemanding, uncomplicated
   hard, arduous, formidable, problematic
   old, mature, passé, established
   new, innovative, current, inventive
   right, accurate, justifiable, precise
   wrong, erroneous, flawed, misguided
   dark, murky, sinister, forbidding
   light, radiant, luminous, incandescent
   happy, elated, jubilant, euphoric
   sad, poignant, heartrending, sorrowful

PLAY THE GAME

1. For each player in the group, use one set of synonyms: 4 sets of synonyms (16 cards) for four players; 5 sets of synonyms (20 cards) for five players; 6 sets of synonyms (24 cards) for six players.

2. Mix up and deal out all the cards. Each player gets 4 cards.

3. Players keep their cards hidden from the others as they organize their hand, looking for synonyms. Then each player selects a card to discard.

4. Players place their unwanted cards facedown on the table. When all players are ready, they slide their discard to the player on their left at the same time.

5. The first player to get four synonyms slaps his or her cards down on the table. To secure the win, the player must use each word correctly in a different sentence.

Name _____   Date _____

Hidden Synonyms

Hidden in the definitions is a common overused synonym for the words in italics. Unscramble the boldface letters to spell the overused word.

1. Something that is *coarse* is uneven and not smoot**h**. Coarse also describes someone who lacks manners. A *jagged* edge is uneven with sharp points. *Irregular* describes something that is uneven in shape, position, or rate (like an irregular heartbeat); something irregular is not uniform or straight.

   Coarse, jagged, and *irregular* are synonyms for ____ ____ ____ ____ ____ .

2. Something *rigid* is stiff and fixed and will not move. When something is *inflexible* it is not e**a**sily bent, **ch**anged or altered. An object can be inflexible. A person can be inflexible, too—for example, about bedtime. An inflexible person is *unbending*, and will not bend, yield or give in to outside influences no matter what.

   Rigid, inflexible, and *unbending* are synonyms for ____ ____ ____ ____ .

3. Someone **w**ho is **s**accharine is excessively sugary in attitude, tone, or character. Gentle emotions that are caring and loving are soft and **t**ender. A tenderhearted person might take in stray dogs and cats. **S**entim**e**ntal feelings exaggerate romance or sadness.

   Saccharine, tender, and *sentimental* are synonyms for: ____ ____ ____ ____ ____ .

4. Something or s**o**meone *tranquil* is calm, steady, unruffled. Something t**h**at is **s**upple **m**oves with ease and grace. As a character trait, a supple mind adapts easily. To be steady, reliable, and dependable is to be c**o**nsistent. When **s**omeone or something is consistent, it means there will be no upsets, no surprises.

   Tranquil, supple, and *consistent* are synonyms for: ____ ____ ____ ____ ____ ____ .

5. A sharp, biting, critical pers**o**n is *acerbic*. Someone who is *embitte**r**ed* is miserable, disillusioned, and full of resentment. Acerbic and embittered people are *di**s**agreeable* since they are **u**npleasant, bad-tempered, and often nasty.

   Acerbic, embittered, and *disagreeable* are synonyms for: ____ ____ ____ ____ .

Select two of the hidden words. Write a sentence using each word and underline the word. Then rewrite each sentence using a more interesting and exact synonym.

_____

_____

_____

_____

Name _____   Date _____

Synonym Substitution

Write a more descriptive synonym for the overused word in brackets.

1. No one liked her *[sweet]* ____ ____ _c_ ____ ____ ____ ____ ____ ____ ____ tone of voice, especially when she used baby talk with her little dog.

2. Mr. H was so *[hard]* ____ ____ ____ _l_ ____ ____ ____ ____ ____ ____ about school uniform rules that he sent me home because my belt wasn't blue!

3. To ensure a *[smooth]* ____ ____ ____ _s_ ____ ____ ____ ____ ____ ____ texture, free of lumps, the chef put the pudding in a blender.

4. He has been *[sour]* ____ ____ ____ ____ ____ ____ ____ ____ _a_ ____ ____ ____ to work with or be around ever since he did not get that promotion.

5. The *[rough]* ____ ____ ____ ____ ____ ____ ____ _a_ ____ cobblestone made it difficult to push the baby carriage.

Write sentences for two of your answers.

_____

_____

Draw a picture to illustrate one of your sentences.

Name _____   Date _____

Crossword Puzzle

Read the clues. Use synonyms for words in the box to complete the puzzle.

> **SYNONYMS** *hard, rough, smooth, sour, sweet*

CLUES

ACROSS

1. Dancers have _____ bodies.
4. Slavery _____ the people in bondage.
5. Exaggeratedly emotional feelings
8. Critical, sharp, and cutting
9. Unmoving and unchangeable
10. The rough fabric was _____ and itchy

DOWN

2. Stiff and inflexible
3. Calm and serene
6. Uneven, like a coastline with inlets and bays
7. Gentle, soft, and loving

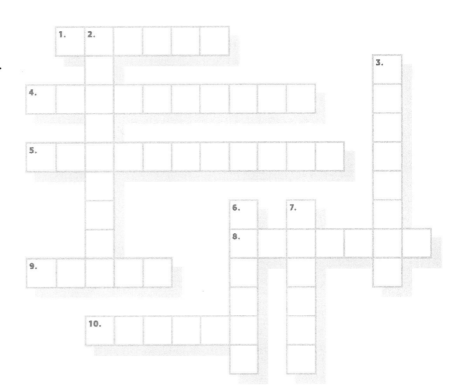

On the back, write and illustrate a sentence using one of your answers. Use any verb tense.

Name _____   Date _____

Word Cards

▸ **Write the meaning for each synonym.**

▸ **Add other synonyms for the word.**

▸ **Cut out the cards and tape or staple them to index cards.**

▸ **Write a sentence for one of the synonyms on the back of the card.**

SYNONYMS FOR *hard*

1. *inflexible* means _____

2. *rigid* means _____

3. *unbending* means _____

4. Other words I know for *hard*:

_____

_____

_____

SYNONYMS FOR *rough*

1. *coarse* means _____

2. *irregular* means _____

3. *jagged* means _____

4. Other words I know for *rough*:

_____

_____

_____

SYNONYMS FOR *smooth*

1. *consistent* means _____

2. *supple* means _____

3. *tranquil* means _____

4. Other words I know for *smooth*:

_____

_____

_____

SYNONYMS FOR *sour*

1. *acerbic* means _____

2. *disagreeable* means _____

3. *embittered* means _____

4. Other words I know for *sour*:

_____

_____

_____

SYNONYMS FOR *sweet*

1. *saccharine* means _____

2. *sentimental* means _____

3. *tender* means _____

4. Other words I know for *sweet*:

_____

_____

_____

Name _____   Date _____

Hidden Synonyms

Hidden in the definitions is a common overused synonym for the words in italics. Unscramble the boldface letters to spell the overused word.

1. The booming crash of thunder clouds is *thun**d**erous*. When the volume is so high it might damage your eardrums, causing deafness, it is *deafening*. When the voice of protesters is noisy and lively or angry, it is *v**o**cifero**u**s*.

   Thunderous, deafening, and *vociferous* are synonyms for ____ ____ ____ ____.

2. Something that is *immense* is extremely large. Something *massive* is not just huge in size, it is also heavy and solid. Something *gar**g**antuan,* such as a jumbo jet, has great mass and is **b**ulky.

   Immense, massive, and *gargantuan* are synonyms for ____ ____ ____.

3. Something *di**m**inutive* is tiny in size. *Trivia**l*** means unimportant or having little significance or value. *Lilliputi**a**n* comes from Jonathan **S**wift's *Gulliver's Travels* and describes the people of Lilliput who are about the height of an old-fashioned inkbottle.

   Diminutive, trivial, and *lilliputian* are synonyms for ____ ____ ____ ____ ____.

4. A **s**ound that can barely be heard is *f*aint. Something that is light, sweet, and easy on the ears can be described as *delica**t**e*. Sounds that are not loud or harsh in any way are *mell**o**w*.

   Faint, delicate, and *mellow* are synonyms for ____ ____ ____ ____.

5. Something *l*ofty is of great height. A lofty person has a high opinion of himself and is pompous, arrogant, and snobby. *Eleva**t**ed* describes something raised off the ground. Something that is *coloss**a**l* is so huge in size or force that it inspires fear or wonder.

   Lofty, elevated, and *colossal* are synonyms for ____ ____ ____ ____.

Select two of the hidden words. Write a sentence using each word and underline the word. Then rewrite each sentence using a more interesting and exact synonym.

_____

_____

_____

_____

Name _____   Date _____

Synonym Substitution

Write a more descriptive synonym for the overused word in brackets.

1. The *[big]* ____ ____ _r_ ____ ____ ____ ____ ____ ____ ____ ship, the largest ever built, set sail on its first 'round-the-world cruise.

2. The *[tall]* ____ ____ _l_ ____ ____ ____ ____ ____ Burj Khalifa Tower in Dubai is now the world's record-holder, with a height of 2,717 feet.

3. Unlike the loud, blaring sounds of the city, the sounds of the country are gentle and *[soft]* ____ ____ ____ ____ _o_ ____ .

4. The *[loud]* ____ ____ _c_ ____ ____ ____ ____ ____ ____ ____ protest outside city hall could be heard half a mile away.

5. The fancy restaurant's *[small]* ____ ____ ____ ____ ____ ____ ____ ____ _v_ ____ portions were tasty but not filling, so we made sandwiches when we got home.

Write sentences for two of your answers.

_____

_____

Draw a picture to illustrate one of your sentences.

Name _____   Date _____

Crossword Puzzle

Read the clues. Use synonyms for words in the box to complete the puzzle.

SYNONYMS *big, loud, small, soft, tall*

CLUES

ACROSS

4. Like the miniature teacups in a dollhouse

7. Small and unimportant

9. The _____ screams of fans made it impossible to hear the band.

10. An arrogant, snobby manner.

DOWN

1. A light, sweet sound is this.

2. The _____ train tracks were right outside his fifth-floor living room.

3. A word that describes a large structure, like a monolith

5. The size of a stadium that holds an extremely large number of people

6. Clapping, shouting, and stamping feet make this kind of applause.

8. Barely audible

**On the back, write
and illustrate a sentence
using one of your answers.
Use any verb tense.**

Word Cards

▸ **Write the meaning for each synonym.**

▸ **Add other synonyms for the word.**

▸ **Cut out the cards and tape or staple them to index cards.**

▸ **Write a sentence for one of the synonyms on the back of the card.**

SYNONYMS FOR big

1. *gargantuan* means _____
2. *immense* means _____
3. *massive* means _____
4. Other words I know for *big*:

_____

_____

_____

SYNONYMS FOR loud

1. *deafening* means _____
2. *thunderous* means _____
3. *vociferous* means _____
4. Other words I know for *loud*:

_____

_____

_____

SYNONYMS FOR small

1. *diminutive* means _____
2. *lilliputian* means _____
3. *trivial* means _____
4. Other words I know for *small*:

_____

_____

_____

SYNONYMS FOR soft

1. *delicate* means _____
2. *faint* means _____
3. *mellow* means _____
4. Other words I know for *soft*:

_____

_____

_____

SYNONYMS FOR tall

1. *colossal* means _____
2. *elevated* means _____
3. *lofty* means _____
4. Other words I know for *tall*:

_____

_____

_____

Review Game 4: Fiction Word Hunt

SKILL Finding synonyms in fiction
NUMBER OF PLAYERS Pairs
OBJECT OF THE GAME To use synonyms to describe characters and details in fiction
MATERIALS Each student's current free-choice reading or favorite fiction book, and set of Word Cards for Units 7 and 8 (pages 40 and 44)

HOW TO PLAY

1. Pair up students who select the same book or books on similar topics. Players review their word cards and look in the book for characters, events, or details that can be described using the synonyms.

2. Players write the title and author of the book at the top of a piece of paper. Have them note the page number where a description of the character or event can be found. Then have them write a sentence (or sentences) using one or more words from the units.

   Example 1
   Harry Potter and the Sorcerer's Stone, by J. K. Rowling
   page ____; Hagrid is a ***gargantuan*** person, who looks ***coarse***, but is really quite ***sentimental***.

   Example 2
   Harry Potter and the Sorcerer's Stone, by J. K. Rowling
   page ____; Hagrid is a ***gargantuan*** person.
   His appearance is ***coarse***.
   Hagrid is surprisingly ***sentimental***, especially about magical creatures.

3. Teams score 1 point for each synonym used and a bonus point for using more than one of the synonyms in a single sentence. The single sentence in example 1 scores 3 points for using three synonyms, and 2 more points for using two additional words in a single sentence. Example 2 earns 3 points for using 3 words, one in each sentence.

4. At the end of the time allotted, the pair with the highest score wins.

Name _____   Date _____

Hidden Synonyms

Hidden in the definitions is a common overused synonym for the words in italics. Unscramble the boldface letters to spell the overused word.

1. Something that occurs at the beginning happens *initially*. The way an event first occurs is how it happens *originally*. Something that is ahead of all others in rank, position, or importance is *foremost*.

   Initially, originally, and *foremost* are synonyms for ___ ___ ___ ___ ___.

2. What is about to be mentioned or comes after is the *following* item. Something that follows in time or order happens *subsequently*. What happens later in time, but not exactly right after, happens *afterward*.

   Following, subsequently, and *afterward* are synonyms for ___ ___ ___ ___.

3. The end result, especially after a long delay, is what happens *finally*. What *ultimately* occurs, happens eventually, in the end, and after all else. A series of events that leads to or shows something unmistakably is *conclusive*.

   Finally, ultimately, and *conclusive* are synonyms for ___ ___ ___ ___.

4. Something fairly close to correct is *approximately* right. When something is more or less or around a certain amount or time (but not as close as approximately), it may **be** *roughly* correct. Something that will happen in the near future is an *approaching* event.

   Approximately, roughly, and *approaching* are synonyms for ___ ___ ___ ___ ___.

5. Something that happens now and then, or from *ti***m**e to time, happens *occasionally*. Events that occur without a pattern or order in ti**m**e happen *sporadically*. Things that happen *infrequently* are rar**e** and do not occur of**t**en.

   Occasionally, sporadically, and *infrequently* are synonyms for

   ___ ___ ___ ___ ___ ___ ___ ___ ___.

Select two of the hidden words. Write a sentence using each word and underline the word. Then rewrite each sentence using a more interesting and exact synonym.

_____

_____

_____

_____

Name _____   Date _____

Synonym Substitution

Write a more descriptive synonym for the overused word in brackets.

1. *[Sometimes]* ____ ____ ____ *a* ____ ____ ____ ____ ____ ____ ____ ____ the coach
   would treat us to pizza after a good practice, but we could never guess when.

2. *[First]* ____ ____ ____ ____ ____ ____ ____ _*l*_ ____ ____, the school was exclusively
   for girls, but in 1972 it began accepting boys, too.

3. The show is *[about]* ____ ____ _*p*_ ____ ____ ____ ____ ____ ____ ____ ____
   an hour and a half, so we can meet you at 7:00.

4. The whistle blew. *[Next]* ____ ____ ____ *s* ____ ____ ____ ____ ____ ____ ____
   a time-out was called.

5. *[Last]* ____ ____ ____ ____ *m* ____ ____ ____ ____ ____ , the good guys will win, the
   bad guys will be banished, and people will all live happily ever after.

Write sentences for two of your answers.

_____

_____

Draw a picture to illustrate one of your sentences.

Name _____   Date _____

Crossword Puzzle

Read the clues. Use synonyms for words in the box to complete the puzzle.

> **SYNONYMS** *about, first, last, next, sometimes*

CLUES

ACROSS

1. In the championship playoffs, our 8-to-1 victory was _____.

4. Not happening often or on a schedule

5. Oncoming, dark clouds warned us a storm was _____.

7. More or less, or just about

9. The _____ announcement applies to everyone, so listen carefully.

10. Many actors only work _____ and need to have a day job.

DOWN

2. Happening at the beginning

3. Ahead of or above all others in importance

6. Happening later

8. At the end or in conclusion, like a summary

> **On the back, write and illustrate a sentence using one of your answers. Use any verb tense.**

Name _____   Date _____

Word Cards

▶ **Write the meaning for each synonym.**

▶ **Add other synonyms for the word.**

▶ **Cut out the cards and tape or staple them to index cards.**

▶ **Write a sentence for one of the synonyms on the back of the card.**

SYNONYMS FOR *about*

1. *approaching* means _____
2. *approximately* means _____
3. *roughly* means _____
4. Other words I know for *about*:

_____

_____

_____

SYNONYMS FOR *first*

1. *foremost* means _____
2. *initially* means _____
3. *originally* means _____
4. Other words I know for *first*:

_____

_____

_____

SYNONYMS FOR *last*

1. *conclusive* means _____
2. *finally* means _____
3. *ultimately* means _____
4. Other words I know for *last*:

_____

_____

_____

SYNONYMS FOR *next*

1. *afterward* means _____
2. *following* means _____
3. *subsequently* means _____
4. Other words I know for *next*:

_____

_____

_____

SYNONYMS FOR *sometimes*

1. *infrequently* means _____
2. *occasionally* means _____
3. *sporadically* means _____
4. Other words I know for *sometimes*:

_____

_____

_____

Name _____   Date _____

Hidden Synonyms

Hidden in the definitions is a common overused synonym for the words in italics. Unscramble the boldface letters to spell the overused word.

1. The *basis* is the base on which an argument or explanation rests. It is the underlying **c**ircumstance or condition. A *motive* is the reason behind an action. The *grounds* are the knowledge, beliefs, or events that make up the foundation for what happens.

Basis, motive and *grounds* are synonyms for ____ ____ ____ ____ ____.

2. Things or ideas that are totally dissimilar or separate are *disparate*. Ideas or arguments that are **d**iv**e**rg**e**nt disagree—they diverge or go o**ff** in opposite directions. Opposite opinions are c**o**ntradictory.

Disparate, divergent and *contradictory* are synonyms for

____ ____ ____ ____ ____ ____ ____ ____ ____.

3. The *outcome* is the result of what happens. The outcome of a rookie's first game is important. The **c**ons**e**quence is what **f**ollows from a given action. The consequences of playing well or poorly will determine whether the rookie stays or goes back to the minors. The *upshot* is the **f**inal result. The *upshot* of the great play he made means he stays in the majors.

Outcome, consequence, and *upshot* are synonyms for ____ ____ ____ ____ ____ ____.

4. Things that are *essential* are fundamentally necessary. Something that is *vital* is most u**r**gently needed, for exam**p**le, medical aid after an earthquake. **M**om**ento**us describes something that is outstandingly significant.

Essential, vital, and *momentous* are synonyms
for ____ ____ ____ ____ ____ ____ ____ ____ ____.

5. Things that are *equivalent* are equal or have the same value. Things that are *comparable* are easily compared because they are alike in k**i**nd, quality, quantity, or degree. Things that are **a**nalogou**s** to each other are related, parallel, or resemble each other in some way.

Comparable, equivalent, and *analogous* are synonyms for ____ ____ ____ ____ ____ ____.

Select two of the hidden words. Write a sentence using each word and underline the word. Then rewrite each sentence using a more interesting and exact synonym.

_____

_____

_____

_____

Name _____   Date _____

Synonym Substitution

Write a more descriptive synonym for the overused word in brackets.

1. Barack Obama was elected President of the United States in 2008. It was a
   [important] ____ ____ ____ ____ _n_ ____ ____ ____ ____ event in U.S. history.

2. The *[effect]* ____ ____ ____ _s_ ____ ____ ____ ____ ____ ____ ____ of not studying
   may be failing the course.

3. From what I see on the map, the directions you gave me are
   [different] ____ ____ ____ ____ ____ ____ ____ ____ ____ ____ ____ _r_ ____.

4. There are many arduous swimming events at the Olympics, but none is
   [similar] ____ _n_ ____ ____ ____ ____ ____ ____ ____ to running the marathon.

5. On what *[cause]* ____ ____ ____ _u_ ____ ____ ____ do you think the club should not
   include people from other schools?

Write sentences for two of your answers.

_____

_____

Draw a picture to illustrate one of your sentences.

Name _____   Date _____

Crossword Puzzle

Read the clues. Use synonyms for words in the box to complete the puzzle.

> **SYNONYMS** *cause, different, effect, important, similar*

CLUES

ACROSS

1. She disagreed because she reached a _____ conclusion.

4. The final result

7. On equal or similar terms

10. Necessary

DOWN

2. Six eggs and half a dozen eggs are this.

3. Broadly varied, distinct

5. They were so far ahead, the _____ of the game was never in doubt.

6. Day workers are paid on a daily _____.

8. The cause for an action

9. Extremely important

> On the back, write
> and illustrate a sentence
> using one of your answers.
> Use any verb tense.

Name _____   Date _____

Word Cards

▸ **Write the meaning for each synonym.**

▸ **Add other synonyms for the word.**

▸ **Cut out the cards and tape or staple them to index cards.**

▸ **Write a sentence for one of the synonyms on the back of the card.**

SYNONYMS FOR *cause*

1. *basis* means _____
2. *grounds* means _____
3. *motive* means _____
4. Other words I know for *cause*:

_____

_____

_____

SYNONYMS FOR *different*

1. *contradictory* means _____
2. *disparate* means _____
3. *divergent* means _____
4. Other words I know for *different*:

_____

_____

_____

SYNONYMS FOR *effect*

1. *consequence* means _____
2. *outcome* means _____
3. *upshot* means _____
4. Other words I know for *effect*:

_____

_____

_____

SYNONYMS FOR *important*

1. *essential* means _____
2. *momentous* means _____
3. *vital* means _____
4. Other words I know for *important*:

_____

_____

_____

SYNONYMS FOR *similar*

1. *analogous* means _____
2. *comparable* means _____
3. *equivalent* means _____
4. Other words I know for *similar*:

_____

_____

_____

Review Game 5: Cloze Concentration

SKILL Use synonyms to complete sentences
NUMBER OF PLAYERS Pairs
OBJECT OF THE GAME Find the word that completes a cloze sentence.
MATERIALS Students' Word Cards, Blank game cards (page 62),
bag for each pair of students

MAKE THE GAME CARDS

1. Duplicate and distribute four pages of blank game cards (page 62). Players cut the cards into strips, so that the word and sentence cards are still attached.

2. Pairs of players place one set of Word Cards for Units 9 and 10 in a bag. Then they take turns, each taking nine words out of the bag and copying the word on the left side of a blank game card. On both parts of the remaining four blank game cards, write: "Wild Card."

3. On the right sentence side of the card, players write a cloze sentence for the word. Where the target word would appear in the sentence, have students draw a box:

ORIGINALLY	We live in San Diego, but we are [ ] from St. Louis.

4. Students review each other's words and sentences to be sure they are correct. Then have students cut apart the game cards. Each pair of students should have made a total of 40 game cards: 18 sets of word-and-cloze sentence cards and four Wild Cards. Place each pair's game cards in an envelope. Have students write their initials in the top right corner of the envelope. Collect the envelopes.

PLAY THE GAME

1. Randomly distribute the envelopes, making sure that no pair gets its own set of game cards. Players mix up the cards and place them facedown in a 5 x 8 array.

2. Play Concentration. The first player turns over two cards. If the cards show a word and a cloze sentence that the word completes, the player then gives the meaning of the vocabulary word. If correct, the player keeps the cards. Then it is the second player's turn. Note: If the player turns over a Wild Card, he or she may write a vocabulary word or a sentence to make a pair.

3. If the cards don't match, or if the player cannot correctly define the word, the cards are turned facedown again and the second player takes a turn.

4. When no cards are left facedown, the player with the most cards wins.

Bonus Review Game: Synonym Pyramid

SKILL Finding synonym pairs

NUMBER OF PLAYERS Individuals or pairs

OBJECT OF THE GAME Match the cards in the pyramid with synonyms

MATERIALS 40 blank game cards (page 62) or index cards

MAKE THE GAME CARDS

1. Choose any two units and write all overused words and their three synonyms on 40 blank game cards (page 62) or 40 index cards. If using Units 5 or 6, you will need extra blank cards.

2. Write the words along the short side of the cards.

3. Turn the cards facedown and mix well.

MAKE THE PYRAMID

1. Gather the cards into a deck, facedown.

2. Turn over the top card and place it on the table.

3. Turn over the next 2 cards and place them in the second row, slightly overlapping the first card. *Be sure the words on the cards are visible.*

4. Place the next 3 cards in the third row, slightly overlapping the row above.

5. Repeat, adding four cards to row 4, five cards to row 5, and six cards to row 6. The array should resemble a pyramid.

6. Hold the remaining 19 cards facedown in your hand.

PLAY THE GAME

1. The cards that are not covered by other cards are free cards. These cards are available to match.

2. Look for synonyms in the bottom row. Remove synonym pairs.

3. When all available matches have been made, turn over the top card of the remaining cards in your hand. If it can be matched to a free card, remove the synonym pair from the game.

4. If the card does not match a free card, place it faceup to start a discard pile. Turn over the next card from the facedown deck. Try to match it to a free card in the pyramid or the top card in the faceup discard pile. Note: When playing in pairs, the next player takes a turn when the first player has made all available matches with one card from the facedown deck.

5. The player with the most pairs of synonyms wins. Mix up all the cards to play again.

Word Graphs: Denotation/Connotation
USE WITH UNITS 1 THROUGH 6

INTRODUCE DENOTATION AND CONNOTATION

Begin by explaining that the denotation of a word is its dictionary meaning: *say* means to speak. Then discuss that words may also have connotations, meanings that are implied, usually depending on the context. Connotations can be positive, negative, or neutral. For example: explain that *say* is neutral, neither positive nor negative. *Shout* can be positive—if you are shouting for joy when a goal is scored. *Shout* can also be negative—if you are loudly disagreeing with the umpire's call. The connotation of a word depends on context, how the word is used.

INTRODUCE WORD GRAPHS

Draw a large rectangle on the board with a diagonal line, similar to the Word Graph reproducible on the next page. Write "Positive" on the upper half, and "Negative" on the lower half. Then write the word *say* next to a point in the center of the diagonal neutral line. Explain that it is neutral, neither positive nor negative. Ask students to suggest synonyms for *say* that are positive, for example, *exclaim*, and negative, such as *cry*. Have them use their suggested words in sentences that illustrate the connotation. For more practice, discuss and add these words to a graph: *okay, happy, fine, sad,* and *miserable*. Ask students to decide which ones are positive, which are negative, and which words should be closest to the neutral line.

USING WORD GRAPHS

1. Duplicate and distribute one word graph to each student or to pairs of students.

2. Students pick two overused words from the units they are working with, and write a sentence for each synonym, underlining the target word.

3. Next, students plot their synonyms on the graph, deciding whether the words are positive, negative, or neutral (on the line).

4. Allow small groups to compare graphs and discuss placement (connotation) of words.

Name _____   Date _____

Word Graphs: Denotation/Connotation

Pick two overused words from each unit. Write sentences for the synonyms. Underline synonyms. Then plot the overused words and their synonyms on the graph.

+ Positive

– Negative

1. _____
2. _____
3. _____
4. _____
5. _____
6. _____
7. _____
8. _____
9. _____
10. _____
11. _____
12. _____

Comic Strip Conventions
USE WITH UNIT 9 TOGETHER WITH OTHER UNITS

INTRODUCE COMIC STRIP CONVENTIONS: SPEECH AND THOUGHT BUBBLES, INTRODUCTORY AND TRANSITIONAL BOXES

Show students some favorite multi-panel comic strips from newspapers that include dialogue and thought bubbles and introductory and transitional text in boxes. Explain each convention, noting in particular the differences in design between speech and thought bubbles.

Speech bubbles are usually smooth shapes with sharp "points" aimed at the speaker.

Thought bubbles have rounded, billowy edges and soft bubbles of decreasing size that indicate the thinker.

Introductory & Transitional Text Boxes Introductory boxes are at the top of cartoon panels. Transitional text boxes are at the bottom.

Point out transition words (Unit 9) and other targeted vocabulary. Explain that the information that goes in the boxes determines where it is placed in the panel. Help students see that the boxes at the top of frames provide introductory or background information needed to understand what will happen in the panels. Boxed text along the bottom of a frame provides a transition to the next panel, or provides a short summary at the end.

USING COMICS

1. Duplicate and distribute page 59. Have students use their Unit 9 Transition Synonyms Word Cards for reference.

2. Place cards with numbers 1 through 8 in a bag. Have students select two or three cards at random. These are the units they can choose words from for their comics and stories, along with the transition words from Unit 9. Due to the limited amount of space in the panels, students may use the most appropriate or shortest synonym for the comic. (They will use additional and more interesting synonyms in their stories.)

3. Encourage students to use at least one of each convention—speech bubbles, thought bubbles, and introductory and transition boxes—in the panels.

4. Below the comic, have students write a narrative story using the word cards they chose. Have them underline each vocabulary word in their story.

Name _____   Date _____

Comic Strip Conventions

_____

_____

_____

_____

_____

_____

_____

_____

_____

_____

_____

"Picture This" Call-Outs
Use With Units 1 Through 10

INTRODUCE CALL-OUTS

Review or introduce comic conventions: speech and thought bubbles, and introductory and transitional boxes. (See page 58.) Show students a newspaper or magazine photograph. Discuss what the people in the picture might be saying to each other or to the reader. Have students suggest interesting synonyms for *said, told,* or *answered.* Repeat for what the people might be thinking. Then brainstorm text for an introductory box to tell readers what they need to know that led up to this photograph. Repeat to create text for a transition box about what might happen next, or for a summary.

USING "PICTURE THIS" CALL-OUTS

1. Have students bring in their own newspaper or magazine photograph of two or more people and tape it to a piece of writing paper. Photos can include animals.

2. Duplicate and distribute a page of call-outs (speech and thought bubbles) and boxes for students to cut out and tape to the photographs. (See page 61.)

3. Have students use their Transition and Essay Synonym Word Cards (from Units 9 and 10) to help them write text for top introductory or background boxes and for bottom transition or summary boxes.

4. Encourage them to use their Synonym Word Cards from other units to write text for at least one speech and one thought bubble.

5. On the writing paper, students write a story to go with their photograph. Give extra credit for each interesting synonym used in call-outs and stories.

"Picture This" Call-Outs

Word Cards
See directions for review games on pages 18, 27, 36, 45, 54, and 55.

Unit 1

PAGE 10
1. say, 2. tell, 3. ask, 4. yell, 5. answer

PAGE 11
1. screeched, 2. cautioned, 3. countered, 4. declared, 5. inquired

PAGE 12
Across: 2. announced, 5. implore, 6. assert, 9. profess, 10. bellow
Down: 1. rant, 3. opine, 4. remark, 7. retort, 8. beseech

Unit 2

PAGE 14
1. awesome, 2. beautiful, 3. perfect, 4. awful, 5. unfair

PAGE 15
1. horrendous, 2. exquisite, 3. impressive, 4. unwarranted, 5. flawless

PAGE 16
Across: 1. fabulous, 4. inequitable, 7. appealing, 8. indefensible, 10. ideal
Down: 2. alluring, 3. faultless, 5. excellent, 6. tragic, 9. dire

Unit 3

PAGE 19
1. go, 2. take, 3. give, 4. want, 5. think

PAGE 20
1. contemplated, 2. bestow, 3. captured, 4. advance, 5. yearned.

PAGE 21
Across: 4. reflect, 5. grasp, 7. ensued, 8. aspire, 10. covet
Down: 1. deem, 2. seize, 3. furnish, 6. persist, 9. equip

Unit 4

PAGE 23
1. boring, 2. nice, 3. like, 4. very, 5. get

PAGE 24
1. congenial, 2. appreciated, 3. profoundly, 4. tedious, 5. obtain

PAGE 25
Across: 7. commonplace, 8. perceive, 9. relish, 10. banal
Down: 1. savor, 2. deeply, 3. exceedingly, 4. gracious, 5. acquire, 6. amiable

Unit 5

PAGE 28
1. good, 2. easy, 3. bad, 4. hard, 5. old, 6. new

PAGE 29
1. straightforward, 2. beneficial, 3. problematic, 4. established, 5. current, 6. injurious

PAGE 30
Across: 2. undemanding, 3. arduous, 10. innovative, 11. inventive, 12. mature
Down: 1. uncomplicated, 4. formidable, 5. passé, 6. horrific, 7. appalling, 8. respectable, 9. competent

Unit 6

PAGE 32
1. right, 2. wrong, 3. dark, 4. light, 5. happy, 6. sad

PAGE 33
1. heartrending, 2. euphoric, 3. forbidding, 4. luminous, 5. justifiable, 6. erroneous

PAGE 34
Across: 3. accurate, 7. sinister, 9. flawed, 10. jubilant, 11. elated, 12. poignant
Down: 1. incandescent, 2. murky, 4. sorrowful, 5. misguided, 6. precise, 8. radiant

Answer Key

Unit 7

PAGE 37
1. rough, 2. hard, 3. sweet, 4. smooth, 5. sour

PAGE 38
1. saccharine, 2. inflexible, 3. consistent,
4. disagreeable, 5. irregular

PAGE 39
Across: 1. supple, 4. embittered,
5. sentimental, 8. acerbic, 9. rigid, 10. coarse
Down: 2. unbending, 3. tranquil,
6. jagged, 7. tender

Unit 8

PAGE 41
1. loud, 2. big, 3. small, 4. soft, 5. tall

PAGE 42
1. gargantuan, 2. colossal, 3. mellow,
4. vociferous, 5. diminutive

PAGE 43
Across: 4. lilliputian, 7. trivial,
9. deafening, 10. lofty
Down: 1. delicate, 2. elevated, 3. massive,
5. immense, 6. thunderous, 8. faint

Unit 9

PAGE 46
1. first, 2. next, 3. last, 4. about, 5. sometimes

PAGE 47
1. occasionally, 2. originally, 3. approximately,
4. subsequently, 5. ultimately

PAGE 48
Across: 1. conclusive, 4. infrequently,
5. approaching, 7. roughly,
9. following, 10. sporadically
Down: 2. initially, 3. foremost,
6. afterward, 8. finally

Unit 10

PAGE 50
1. cause, 2. different, 3. effect,
4. important, 5. similar

PAGE 51
1. momentous, 2. consequence,
3. contradictory, 4. analogous, 6. grounds.

PAGE 52
Across: 1. divergent, 4. upshot,
7. comparable, 10. essential
Down: 2. equivalent, 3. disparate, 5. outcome,
6. basis, 8. motive, 9. vital

Professional Resources

Beck, I., McKeown, M., & Kucan, L. (2002).
Bringing words to life. New York: Guilford Press.

Feldman, K., Kinsella, K. (2004) *Narrowing the language gap: The case for explicit vocabulary instruction.* New York: Scholastic Inc.

National Reading Panel (2003). *Put Reading First: The Research Building Blocks of Reading Instruction* (Second Edition), Washington, DC: The Partnership for Reading, National Institute for Literacy.

READ 180 Stage C Rbook Stage C, Teacher's Edition (2005). New York: Scholastic, Inc.

Stahl, S. (Spring 2003). Words are learned incrementally over multiple exposures. *American Educator,* 18-19.

Stahl, S. & Fairbanks, M. (1986). The effects of vocabulary instruction: A model-based meta-analysis. *Review of Educational Research,* 56(1), 72-110.